U.S. General Services Administration

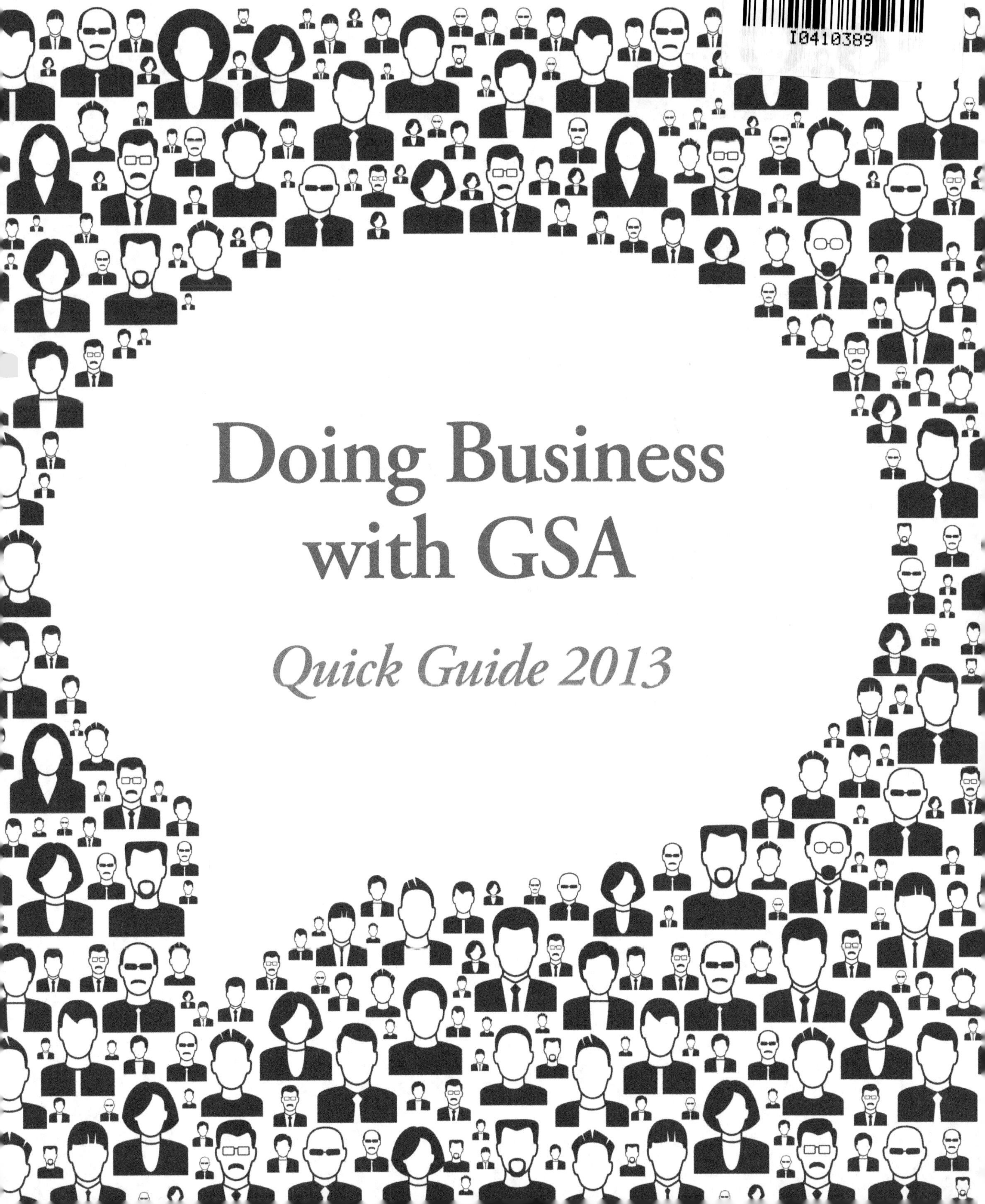

Doing Business with GSA

Quick Guide 2013

Small Business Community:

The General Services Administration's Office of Small Business Utilization team would like to introduce you to the *2013 Doing Business with GSA Quick Guide*.

Each year we look to small businesses like you to determine how we can make this publication more useful. In response to your need for less paper and more sustainable resources, we have streamlined our 2012 version of this publication into an easy-to-read road map. This guide will take you through GSA's electronic resources to find the business opportunities available for your company.

We hope you find it helpful and we wish you much success as you continue to partner with our agency.

Jiyoung Park
Associate Administrator
The Office of Small Business Utilization
General Services Administration

Three Easy Steps

Step One: The Quick Guide is a Road Map.

It's best to think of the *Quick Guide* as an easy-to-read road map that can guide you through the GSA web site to find the business opportunities available to your company. Like all good road maps, the *Quick Guide* won't have a lot of words or directions. Instead, the Guide will tell you where to find more information at the *GSA.gov* web site.

Step Two: Charting a Path

On the facing page, the Table of Contents provides you with a dozen "opportunity gateways" that will lead you to more web links where you can find useful information on how to do business with GSA. As a navigational tool, the *Quick Guide* will allow you to map out your own path to the opportunities that await you.

Step Three: Following the Path

Each opportunity gateway has its own page in the booklet. Once you know which one(s) to pursue, just jump to the page(s) to continue your journey. Then, it's just a matter of going to the *GSA.gov* web link(s) to find the information you need. It's that simple.

What to Expect in the Future

We hope you find the *Quick Guide* a useful resource in your search for new opportunities. We will update the *Quick Guide* as new web links are developed and become available.

Thank you for giving us this opportunity to serve you.

Please Note:

While this booklet provides information regarding GSA's contracting vehicles and offers helpful guidance, it should not be construed as a replacement of applicable procurement regulations and policies.

Table of Contents

GSA: For Business

www.gsa.gov/forbusiness

This opportunity gateway features five sections that will lead you to even more information on how GSA and our industry partners work together for the American people. In outline, here is what you'll find at this all-inclusive web page:

Getting Started
- ▶ Getting a Government Contract
- ▶ Tools for GSA Contractors
- ▶ How to Sell to the Government
- ▶ Opportunities for Small Businesses

Supported Programs
- ▶ 21 Gun Salute
- ▶ Ability One
- ▶ Green Proving Ground
- ▶ GSA Vendor Communication Plan
- ▶ Mentor-Protégé
- ▶ Sustainability

Where to Find Help
- ▶ FAS GSA Schedules
- ▶ PBS Industry Relations
- ▶ Office of Small Business Utilization
- ▶ Office of Citizen Services and Innovative Technologies

How GSA Buys
- ▶ Overview
- ▶ Blanket Purchase Agreement (BPA)
- ▶ Government-wide Acquisition Contracts (GWACs)
- ▶ Indefinite Delivery Indefinite Quantity (IDIQ) Contracts
- ▶ Multiple Award Schedules (MAS)
- ▶ Single Awards
- ▶ Small Business Assistance
- ▶ Source Selection

Services that GSA Buys
- ▶ Architecture & Engineering
- ▶ Design & Construction
- ▶ Facilities Maintenance & Management
- ▶ Leasing
- ▶ Green/Energy
- ▶ Information Technology
- ▶ Professional and Technical Solutions
- ▶ Retail Services
- ▶ Childcare
- ▶ Realty Services
- ▶ Real Estate Services
- ▶ Real Property Disposal
- ▶ Travel

GSA SmartPay Charge Cards

www.smartpay.gsa.gov

Accepting the GSA SmartPay charge card is beneficial to your company because you can maximize your ability to capture government sales.

If you already accept these cards from the commercial sector, there is no additional work to do as the GSA SmartPay charge cards operate just like any other corporate charge cards

Most of the SmartPay web page is devoted to information for federal agencies and their employees on how to best use this program to achieve administrative efficiencies.

However, there are important web links for businesses wanting to learn how to take part in this multi-billion dollar marketing opportunity. To find out more, please click on the "Businesses & Vendors" tab at the top right-side of the SmartPay web page.

At the Businesses and Vendors web page, you will learn more about:

- ► How to accept the GSA SmartPay Card.
- ► How to recognize the GSA SmartPay Card.
- ► How your state handles taxes for the GSA SmartPay Card.
- ► Understanding GSA SmartPay Cards

Helpful Hints for Finding SmartPay Cardholders

If you wish to locate and market your products and/or services to SmartPay cardholders you can use Google, or any other search engines, to get web links to federal agencies that maintain public listings of cardholders. For example, to find these free public listings at *Google.com*, please use these search terms:

- ► Government purchase cardholders
- ► FOIA cardholders [FOIA, Freedom of Information Act]

GSA Auctions

www.gsaauctions.gov

What is GSA Auctions?

GSA Auctions offers federal assets ranging from office equipment, to furniture, to vehicles, to land and buildings. GSA Auctions online capabilities allow GSA to offer assets located across the country to any interested buyer, regardless of location.

How to Participate

Participants may choose to browse items that are offered on this site or may choose to search for items and place bids. In order to place a bid(s), participants must register first. To register, please go to the GSA Auctions homepage and click on the register button (or for your convenience, please click, or double click, on this web link):

http://gsaauctions.gov/gsaauctions/gsaauctions/

For More Information

At the bottom of the GSA Auctions homepage are additional web links:

▶ GSA Fleet Vehicle Sales

http://autoauctions.gsa.gov/autoauctions/home.seam

▶ Real Property Disposal

http://realestatesales.gov/gsaauctions/gsaauctions/

Federal Travel

www.gsa.gov/travelindustry

Opportunity Links

At this opportunity gateway, companies can find web links on how to do business with five travel-related programs.

▶ FedRooms – Information for companies interested in providing hotel room inventory to the government:

http://www.gsa.gov/portal/content/105404

▶ Conference Lodging Services – Information for companies interested in providing conference and event services to the government:

http://www.gsa.gov/portal/content/27090

▶ Airline City Pair Program – Information on solicitations for airlines to provide transportation services:

http://www.gsa.gov/portal/category/27075

▶ Travel Services Solutions – A Multiple Award Schedule for contract travel services:

http://www.gsa.gov/portal/category/27054

▶ Transportation Audits – Information for contractors capable of conducting prepayment auditing services for the government:

http://www.gsa.gov/portal/category/27057

Additional Reference Information

This gateway web site also provides links to GSA points of contact, per diem rates, mileage reimbursement rates and the Federal Travel Regulations.

Leading the Way & Opportunities for Businesses

GSA Fleet

http://www.gsa.gov/portal/content/104624

Overview

Since 1954, GSA Fleet has been providing quality vehicles and efficient and economical fleet management services to over 75 participating federal agencies. The GSA Fleet has over 217,000 vehicles and is one of the largest non-tactical federal fleets in the U.S. Government. The GSA Fleet includes:

Automobiles

- ▶ Buses and ambulances
- ▶ Light, medium and heavy trucks
- ▶ Passenger vans
- ▶ Marketing to GSA's Fleet Management Centers

GSA Fleet is supported by a network of Fleet Management Centers (FMCs). To find out more on how your business can support these centers, please go to this web link to find a FMC:

http://www.gsa.gov/portal/category/100759

Business Opportunities with GSA's Maintenance Control Center

The GSA Maintenance Control Center (MCC) handles services requests with vendors located throughout the country. To become a MCC vendor, please go to this web link to get access to the "Vendor Application Letter of Agreement" form.

http://www.gsa.gov/portal/content/104230

Selling Vehicles to GSA Fleet

For more information on how to sell vehicles to GSA Fleet, please go to this web link for the GSA Automotive Center:

http://www.gsa.gov/portal/category/21208

GSA Transportation

www.gsa.gov/transportation

Opportunities for Household Goods Transportation

GSA's Centralized Household Goods Traffic Management Program (CHAMP) assists relocating federal government employees in transporting household goods from one official duty station to another, both domestically and internationally. GSA invites Transportation Service Providers (TSPs) to submit rates in response to Request for Offers during the open filing window. For more information, please go to this web link.

http://www.gsa.gov/portal/content/103864

Opportunities for Freight Management

GSA's Freight Management Program (FMP) provides a framework for fulfilling the domestic freight shipping requirements for federal agencies. To participate in this program, please go to this web link for more information on GSA's Freight Request for Offers.

http://www.gsa.gov/portal/content/110716

Opportunities with GSA Schedule 48

GSA Schedule 48, Transportation, Delivery and Relocation Solutions, provides federal agencies with a variety of transportation services. Specifically, GSA Schedule 48 includes the following services from contractors located across the country:

- ▶ Domestic Express and Ground Routine Shipping,
- ▶ Employee and Office Relocation Services,
- ▶ Local Courier Services,
- ▶ Rental Supplemental Vehicle Program,
- ▶ Transportation Consulting Services, and
- ▶ Ground Passenger Transportation Services.

For more information about GSA Schedule 48, please go to this web link.

http://www.gsaelibrary.gsa.gov/ElibMain/scheduleSummary.do?scheduleNumber=48

Green Power & Utilities

www.gsa.gov/energy

Opportunities Overview

The staff with GSA's Public Utilities Program is a multi-disciplinary team whose mission it is to provide leadership within the federal government with regard to developing contracting vehicles that enable customers to procure utility services at the lowest cost to the taxpayer and the greatest value to the American people.

The team procures for electricity, natural gas, water and sewage services. The current emphasis is on positioning the federal government to take advantage of potential cost savings made possible from restructuring initiatives being pursued by the nation's electric utility industry.

Opportunities Available at GSA's Energy Division Library

In doing business with GSA, all energy utility providers should first visit the GSA Energy Division Library at this web link:

http://www.gsa.gov/portal/content/104187

At this web page, companies will find additional web links to the GSA Area-wide Public Utility Contract Listing, GSA Regional Energy Coordinators and a variety of reference documents on how GSA conducts its procurements.

Opportunities with Green Power

GSA is at the forefront on the federal government's initiatives with Green Power. To find opportunities in how to participate in these programs, please go to this web link:

http://www.gsa.gov/portal/content/100856

Opportunities with GSA Schedule 03 FAC

GSA's offers Energy Management Solutions on GSA Schedule 03 FAC, Facilities Maintenance and Management. For more information about becoming a contractor on GSA Schedule 03 FAC, please go to this web link:

http://www.gsa.gov/portal/content/103128

Real Property Leasing

www.gsa.gov/leasing

Overview

GSA, the nation's largest public real estate organization, provides workspace for more than 1.2 million federal workers through its Public Building Service. GSA manages over 8,100 leases with an annual rent outlay of over $5.5 billion.

GSA leases space in diverse locations when leasing is the best solution for meeting federal space needs. More than 50% of GSA leases are for 10,000 square feet or less. So, there are plenty of opportunities for small businesses interested in this market segment.

Useful Marketing Information

For sub-contracting opportunities with current lessors, GSA posts a monthly, nation-wide lease inventory (in a downloadable Excel spreadsheet format) at its GSA web site. The web link is available at this opportunity gateway web site; but, for your convenience, you can also use this web lin:

http://www.gsa.gov/portal/content/101840

Additional marketing information is available at GSA's Inventory of Owned and Leased Properties at this web link:

http://www.iolp.gsa.gov/iolp/ NationalMap.asp

Opportunities with GSA's National Broker Contractors

GSA's Public Building Service also utilizes the leasing services from four National Broker Contractors. To pursue both sub-contracting and contracting opportunities with these brokers, please go to this web link and click on the "Small Business Points of Contact" file:

http://www.gsa.gov/portal/content/103739

This web link also provides additional reference information about the National Broker Contract.

Indefinite Delivery Indefinite Quantity Contracts

www.gsa.gov/idiq

Overview

Indefinite delivery, indefinite quantity contracts provide for an indefinite quantity of services for a fixed time. They are used when GSA can't determine, above a specified minimum, the precise quantities of supplies or services that the government will require during the contract period. IDIQ's help streamline the contract process and speed service delivery.

IDIQ contracts are most often used for service contracts and architect-engineering services. Awards are usually for one base year with four, one-year option periods.

The government places delivery orders (for supplies) or task orders (for services) against a basic contract for individual requirements. Minimum and maximum quantity limits are specified in the basic contract as either number of units (for supplies) or as dollar values (for services).

Sub-Contracting Opportunities on GSA IDIQ Contracts

GSA provides a nation-wide listing of its IDIQ contractors. The list is available at the opportunity gateway web link provided at the top of this page. The list is in a downloadable Excel spreadsheet format that will allow you to re-organize the information to suit your needs.

To find the point of contact information for the companies listed, please conduct a search at the federal government's *SAM. gov* web site. To find sales information and transactional data on the orders placed against these IDIQ contracts, please type in the GSA contract number into the search box at the *USAspending.gov* web site.

Contracting Opportunities on GSA IDIQ Contracts

To participate in future procurements for GSA's IDIQ contracts please monitor solicitations at the federal government's FedBizOpps web site at this web address:

www.fbo.gov

Telecommunications & Network Services

www.gsa.gov/networkservices

Overview

GSA offers cost-effective contracting solutions for the federal government's communications infrastructure and service needs. GSA services include:

- ▶ Access services
- ▶ Managed network services
- ▶ Network applications
- ▶ Satellite services and applications
- ▶ Telecommunication services
- ▶ Wireless and mobile
- ▶ Accessible telecommunications

Sub-contracting Opportunities

For more information about sub-contracting opportunities with GSA's industry partners, please go to these web links:

Conections II:

http://www.gsa.gov/portal/content/113271

Networx Universal:

http://www.gsa.gov/portal/content/101611

Networx Enterprise:

http://www.gsa.gov/portal/content/101612

SATCOM-II:

http://www.gsa.gov/portal/category/25320

SATCOM Solutions – Small Business

http://www.gsa.gov/portal/content/122231

Contracting Opportunities on GSA Schedule 70

For more information on how to become a contractor on GSA Schedule 70, Information Technology (which includes telecommunication and network services), please go to this web link:

http://www.gsa.gov/portal/content/198693

Government-wide Acquisition Contracts

www.gsa.gov/gwacs

Overview

A Government-wide Acquisition Contract (GWAC) is a pre-competed, multiple-award, indefinite delivery, indefinite quantity (IDIQ) contract that agencies can use to buy total IT solutions. The GWACs managed by GSA provide access to IT solutions such as systems design, software engineering, information assurance, and enterprise architecture solutions.

Sub-contracting Opportunities

For more information about sub-contracting opportunities with GSA's industry partners, please go to these web links:

Alliant:

http://www.gsa.gov/portal/content/103908

Alliant Small Business:

http://www.gsa.gov/portal/content/103417

8(a) STARS II

http://www.gsa.gov/portal/content/208261

VETS:

http://www.gsa.gov/portal/content/102424

Please be aware that there may also be additional sub-contracting opportunities with contractors involved in expired GWACs (on existing task orders) for the next couple of years. To find these opportunities, please go to this web link and click on the web links for the expired GWACs to find the list of industry partners for these programs:

http://www.gsa.gov/portal/category/101715

Contracting Opportunities

Any future GWAC procurement opportunities will be posted on the federal government's FedBizOpps web site at this web address:

www.fbo.gov

Opportunities for over 19,000 Contractors

Federal Supply Schedules

www.gsa.gov/schedulesolicitations

Overview

The GSA Schedules program is the premier acquisition vehicle in the federal government, with approximately $50 billion in yearly spending or 10% of overall federal procurement spending in any one year. For vendors interested in becoming GSA Schedule contractors, they should first visit this web link:

http://www.gsa.gov/portal/category/100635

Sub-contracting Opportunities

With more than 19,000 contractors and about 3,800 contractors with small business sub-contracting plans, there are plenty of sub-contracting opportunities. To get quick access to this list of contractors, please go to this web link:

http://www.gsaelibrary.gsa.gov/ElibMain/scheduleList.do

At this web page, please click on the schedule number to go to that schedule page. At the schedule page, then click on the category number to see a list of contractors. Those contractors identified with an "o" (other than small business) in the socio-economic column have sub-contracting plans where they are obligated to the federal government to sub-contract with small businesses. To get the point of contact information for these companies, please click on the company name.

Contracting Opportunities

The opportunity gateway web site listed above gives direct access to GSA's 31 schedule programs. Just click on the schedule number hypertext links to proceed to the schedule web page.

At the schedule web page, click on the rectangular box labeled "Vendors" to go to the solicitation for that schedule at the federal government's FedBizOpps web page (*www.fbo.gov*).

A Special Note for VA-Managed Federal Supply Schedules

For more information on VA-managed schedules, please go to this web link:

http://www.va.gov/oal/business/fss/schedules.asp

Appendix A: *Frequently Asked Questions*

Who is eligible to use GSA MAS contracts?

The GSA Order ADM 4800.2E, 1/3/2000 identifies eligible users of the GSA MAS contracts:

- ▶ Executive and Other Federal Agencies
- ▶ Mixed-Ownership Government Corporations (Federal Deposit Insurance Corporation (FDIC), Federal Home Loan Banks, etc.)
- ▶ The District of Columbia
- ▶ Cost Reimbursable Government Contractors authorized in writing by a Federal agency (48 CFR 51.1)
- ▶ State and Local Governments through Cooperative and Disaster Recovery Purchasing. www.gsa.gov/cooperativepurchasing

How does GSA determine if vendors are offering prices that are fair and reasonable to Federal Customers?

GSA MAS contracts are negotiated with the goal of obtaining "Most Favored Customer" (MFC) pricing/ discounts. While the MFC is often the vendor's best commercial customer and receives the highest discount, such is not always the case. Per GSAR 538.270(a), "The Government will seek to obtain offeror's best price (the best price given to the most favored customer). However, the Government recognizes that the terms and conditions of commercial sales vary and there may be legitimate reasons why the best price is not achieved." Paragraph

(c) of the GSAR language contains factors that are considered when the Government determines its price negotiation objectives. GSA's goal is to acquire equal to or better than the MFC's discount. (*www.acquisition.gov*)

What is GSA Advantage!® and are all GSA MAS contractors required to participate?

GSA Advantage!® is an online shopping and ordering system that includes products and services under all of the GSA Multiple Award Schedules, Veterans Administration (VA) Schedules and GSA Global Supply items .With over 11 million products and services currently available, electronic ordering through GSAAdvantage!® allows a customer to send an order directly to the GSA Schedule contractor, creating a direct customer-contractor relationship. All GSA Schedule contractors must be registered with GSA Advantage!®To learn more about GSAAdvantage!®, please visit *www.gsaadvantage.gov*.

What is e-Buy?

e-Buy is an online Request for Quotation (RFQ) tool designed to facilitate the request for submission of quotations for a wide range of commercial supplies and services offered by GSA Schedule and Government-wide Acquisition Contract (GWAC) contractors. e-Buy allows Federal agencies (buyers) to maximize their buying power by leveraging the power of the Internet to increase Schedule contractor participation in order to obtain quotations that will result in a best value purchase decision.

e-Buy provides Schedule contractors (sellers) with greater opportunities to offer quotations and increase business volume for supplies and services provided under their Schedule contracts. e-Buy streamlines the buying process with point-and-click functionality by allowing RFQs and responses to be exchanged electronically between Federal agencies and GSA Schedule/GWAC contractors. In short, e-Buy provides both agencies and contractors with a tool that will result in savings of both time and money.

What is a Blanket Purchase Agreement (BPA) under a GSA Schedule contract?

A GSA Schedule BPA is an agreement established by a customer with a GSA Schedule contractor to fill repetitive needs for supplies or services (FAR 8.405-3). It simplifies filling of recurring needs, while leveraging a customer's buying power by taking advantage of quantity discounts, saving administrative time, and reducing paperwork.

A BPA can be set up for use by field offices across the nation, thus allowing them to participate in an agency's BPA and place orders directly with GSA Schedule contractors. In doing so, the entire agency reaps the benefits of additional discounts negotiated into the BPA. A multi-agency BPA is also permitted if the BPA identifies the participating agencies and their estimated requirements at the time the BPA is established. A BPA may be established under a Contractor Team Arrangement.

Some ordering activities are issuing GSA Schedule BPAs for millions of dollars. Is there a dollar amount too large for GSA Schedule BPA procedures? Is there a limit on the dollar value of an order placed against a BPA?

The monetary limitation of a GSA Schedule BPA is determined by the underlying competition conducted by the ordering activity when establishing the BPA. The same ordering procedures outlined in FAR 8.405 apply to the establishment of a GSA Schedule BPA (FAR 8.405-3(a)(2)). Based upon the potential volume of orders under the BPA, ordering activities may be able to obtain greater discounts, regardless of the size of individual orders. The ordering activity shall conduct an annual review of the GSA Schedule BPA to determine whether—

▶ The underlying Schedule contract is still in effect;
▶ The BPA still represents the best value; and
▶ Estimated quantities/amounts have been exceeded and additional price reductions can be obtained.

The ordering activity shall document the results of its review.

What is a Contractor Team Arrangement (CTA) under the GSA MAS Program?

A CTA under the MAS Program is an arrangement in which two or more MAS contractors join together to provide a total solution to meet a customer's needs. Orders placed under a CTA are subject to the terms and conditions of each team member's GSA MAS contract. For more information, please visit *www.gsa.gov/cta*.

Are all products and services offered under GSA Schedule contracts compliant with the Trade Agreements Act?

Yes. All products and services offered under GSA Schedule contracts are evaluated and awarded in accordance with the Trade Agreements Act (FAR 25.4). As an ordering activity contracting officer, can I terminate an order against a Schedule contract? Yes. In accordance with FAR 8.406-4 and 8.406-5, respectively, an ordering activity contracting officer may terminate an order for cause or for the convenience of the government. Such terminations shall comply with FAR 12.403. The GSA Schedule contracting officer shall be notified in all cases where an order has been terminated for cause or fraud is suspected.

What is the Industrial Funding Fee (IFF)?

The IFF is a fee paid by customers to cover GSA's cost of operating the Federal Supply Schedules program. The fee is a percentage of reported sales under Schedules contracts.

How does the Department of Veterans Affairs (VA) provide medical related contracts through the Schedules Program?

Medical Products and Services Schedules are provided under a special agreement. GSA has delegated management responsibility for medical products and services under the Schedules Program to the VA.

The VA Office of Acquisition and Materiel Management (OA&MM) is responsible for establishing, soliciting, awarding, and administering the VA's Federal Supply Schedules Program. VA's Schedules encompass such products as:
- ▶ Pharmaceuticals
- ▶ Medical Equipment And Supplies
- ▶ Dental Supplies
- ▶ X-Ray Equipment And Supplies (Including Medical And Dental X-Ray Film)

- ▶ Patient Mobility Devices (Including Wheelchairs, Scooters, Walkers, etc.)
- ▶ Antiseptic Skin Cleansers
- ▶ Detergents And Soaps
- ▶ Invitro Diagnostics
- ▶ Reagents
- ▶ Test Kits And Sets
- ▶ Clinical Analyzers
- ▶ Laboratory Cost-Per-Test.

For more specific information regarding this program, please contact the VA office. FSS Help Line general questions telephone number (708) 786-7733 or the FSS Service Contract question telephone number (708) 786-7722.

If my business has developed a new product, is GSA a potential customer?

Yes. GSA will evaluate your product to determine if it is new or better than existing items. If the Government needs your product, GSA may negotiate a contract to purchase the product from you. To determine what Schedule is applicable to your commodity, visit *www.gsaelibrary.gsa.gov*.

Is there any system for monitoring how well large prime contractors meet their subcontracting goals?

Yes. Large prime contractors are required to submit reports documenting good faith efforts to meet their subcontracting goals. *www.esrs.gov*

Does the location of my business affect my ability to compete for GSA contracts?

It depends on the solicitation. Solicitations for repair and maintenance and small construction jobs may be limited to the geographic area needing the service. Others, such as solicitations for GSA Supply Catalog items and for large building projects, are open to vendors throughout the United States. In addition, FSS Acquisition Centers handle procurement of the products and services for which they are responsible.

Is it possible to be listed on more than one GSA MAS?

Yes, if you have more than one product or service to sell you are eligible to obtain more than one GSA MAS contract.

How can I learn more about architect/engineer contracting with GSA and other Federal agencies?

GSA's Design Excellence Program booklet gives information on architect/engineer contracting procedures. For a copy or further information on contracting opportunities, please contact:

GSA, Public Buildings Service
Center for Design Excellence and the Arts (PCE)
1800 F Street, NW, Washington, DC 20405

Does GSA use specifications and standards adopted by the private sector?

GSA's policy is to adopt the appropriate specifications and standards of nationally recognized technical organizations, whenever appropriate, and to obtain input from these groups and individual firms on proposed specifications and standards.

Where can I get copies of specifications and standards?

Most solicitations will say where to obtain copies. You may also get copies from the purchasing office that issued the solicitation.

Some of the clauses in my contract seem to be important, but the text of the clauses is missing. What do I do?

When a contract refers to standard clauses listed elsewhere, you still must comply with the clause requirements. The full text of the clauses can be found in the FAR or the GSAM, or you may request a copy of the clauses from the procurement official listed in the solicitation.

What procurements under the simplified acquisition procedures are reserved?

Except for those acquisitions set aside for very small business concerns, each acquisition of products or services that has an anticipated dollar value exceeding $3000, but not over $150,000, is automatically reserved exclusively for small business concerns. It is set aside, unless the contracting officer determines there is not a reasonable expectation of obtaining offers from two or more responsible small businesses that are competitive in terms of market prices, quality and delivery, (see FAR 19.502-2).

Are Request for Proposals (RFPs) always in writing?

No. In emergency situations, GSA may use oral solicitations. Sometimes, when competition is restricted (such as when a purchase must be made from a particular source), a letter RFP is used. Facsimile RFPs are used by some agencies. Eventually, most RFPs and offers will be made via electronic commerce.

Is it necessary that I have electronic commerce/ electronic data interchange (EC/EDI) capability to do business with GSA?

Yes. We pay vendors electronically and in some cases require contractors to provide electronic catalogues.

Appendix B: *Glossary of Terms*

Acquisition Central: Internet website for Government-wide acquisition information.

Blanket Purchase Agreement (BPA): An agreement between the Government and a supplier allowing repetitive purchases during a specified period (see FAR 13.303-1).

Certificate of Competency (COC) Program: The COC Program empowers SBA to certify to Government contracting officers as to all elements of responsibility of any small business to receive and perform a specific Government contract. When the contracting officer determines and documents that an apparent successful small business offeror lacks certain elements of responsibility (including but not limited to, capability, competency, capacity, credit, integrity and limitation on subcontracting), the contracting officer must withhold contract award and refer the matter to the cognizant SBA Government Contracting Area Office serving the area in which the headquarters of the offeror is located (see FAR 19.601(b)).

Commercial Item: Any supply or service, other than real property, that is customarily used for non-Government purposes and that has been sold, leased or licensed to the general public or falls under the additional categories listed in the complete definition of "commercial item" as it appears under FAR 2.101.

Construction Metrication Ombudsman: A senior GSA official responsible for ensuring that GSA is implementing the metric system of measurement in an efficient manner, while ensuring that the goals of the Metric Conversion Act of 1975 are observed.

Cost-Reimbursement Contract: This type of contract provides for payment of allowable incurred costs, to the extent prescribed in the contract. (See FAR 16.3).

Contract: A mutually binding legal relationship obligating the seller to furnish the supplies or services (including construction) and the buyer to pay for them. It includes all types of commitments that obligate the Government to an expenditure of appropriated funds and that, except as otherwise authorized, are in writing. In addition to bilateral instruments, contracts include (but are not limited to) awards and notices of awards; job orders or task letters issued under basic ordering agreements; orders, such as purchase orders, under which the contract becomes effective by written acceptance or performance; and bilateral contract modifications (see FAR 2.101).

Contracting Activity: An element of an agency designated by the agency head and delegated broad authority regarding acquisition functions (see FAR 2.101).

Contracting Officer: A contracting officer has the authority to enter into, administer, and/or terminate contracts. They may also make related determinations and findings (see FAR 2.101).

Delivery Order: An order for supplies placed against an established contract or with Government sources.

Electronic Commerce (EC): Electronic techniques for accomplishing business transactions including electronic mail or messaging, World Wide Web technology, electronic bulletin boards, purchase cards, electronic funds transfer and electronic data interchange (see FAR 2.101).

Electronic Data Interchange (EDI): A technique for electronically transferring and storing formatted information between computers utilizing established and published formats and codes, as authorized by the applicable Federal Information Processing Standards (see FAR 2.101).

Fixed-Price Contract: Contracts that provide for a firm price or, in appropriate cases, an adjustable price. Fixed price contracts providing for an adjustable price may include a ceiling price, a target price (including target cost) or both. Unless otherwise specified in the contract, the ceiling price or the target price is subject to adjustment only by operation of contract clauses providing for equitable adjustment or other revision of the contract price under stated circumstances. The contracting officer shall use firm-fixed- price or fixed-price with economic price adjustment contracts when acquiring commercial items (see FAR 16.201).

Government-wide Commercial Purchase Card: A purchase card, similar in nature to a commercial credit card, issued to authorize agency personnel to use in paying for supplies and services.

Government-wide Point of Entry (GPE): The single point where Government business opportunities greater than $25,000, including synopses of proposed contract actions, solicitations, and associated information, can be accessed electronically by the public. The GPE is located at *http://www.fedbizopps. gov*.

Industry: All concerns primarily engaged in similar lines of activity, as listed and described in the North American Industry Classification System (NAICS).

Information Technology (IT): Any equipment, or interconnected systems(s) or subsystem(s) of equipment used in the automatic acquisition, storage, analysis, evaluation, manipulation, management, movement, control, display, switching, interchange, transmission, or reception of data or information. IT includes computers, ancillary equipment, software, firmware and similar procedures, services and related resources (see FAR 2.101).

North American Industry Classification System (NAICS): The NAICS replaced the Standard Industrial Classification (SIC) Codes. NAICS is an industry classification system used by the statistical agencies of the United States for classifying business establishments. NAICS includes 1,170 industries of which 565 are service based industries.

Negotiation: Exchanges between the Government and offerors, which are undertaken with the intent of allowing the offeror to revise its proposal. Negotiations may include bargaining; i.e., persuasion, alteration of assumptions and positions, and give-and-take, and may apply to price, schedule, technical requirements, type of contract or other terms of a proposed contract.

Offer: A response to a solicitation that, if accepted, would bind the offeror to perform the resultant contract. Responses to invitations for bid (sealed bidding) are offers called "bids" or "sealed bids;" responses to requests for proposals (negotiation) are offers called "proposals;" responses to requests for quotation (negotiation) are not offers and are called "quotations", (see FAR 2.101).

Purchase Order: When issued by the Government, purchase order means an offer by the Government to buy supplies or services, including construction and research and development, upon specified terms and conditions, using simplified acquisition procedures (see FAR 2.101).

Simplified Acquisition Procedures: The methods prescribed in FAR Part 13, for making purchases of products or services (see FAR 2.101).

Small Business Size: SBA's size standards define whether a business entity is small and, thus, eligible for Government programs and preferences reserved for "small business" concerns. Size standards (see FAR 19.1) have been established for types of economic activity, or industry, generally under the NAICS.

Standards: Technical requirements for processes, procedures, practices, and methods that have been adopted as standard.

Statement of Work: A statement of work is a specific statement regarding the requirements needed in a service contract. The statement of work should include all aspects of job requirements, performance, and assessment.

Task Order: An order for services placed against an established contract or with Government sources. (See FAR 2.101).

Appendix C: *Obtaining Grants and Other Support*

A Grant means an award of financial assistance, including cooperative agreements, in the form of money, or property in lieu of money, by the Federal Government to an eligible grantee. GSA does not provide grants to small businesses. However, due to frequent requests for information, we have provided the following helpful resources.

SBA

www.sba.gov/content/what-7j-program y www.sba.gov/financialassistance

Under Section 7(j) of the Small Business Act, SBA is authorized to provide management and technical assistance, through grants and cooperative agreements to qualified service providers. The Agency is not authorized to award grants to assist individuals to start, operate, expand, rebuild, or purchase a business. The management and technical assistance includes specialized training, professional consulting, and executive development. The qualified service providers deliver the training and technical assistance to eligible firms and individuals participating in SBA's Business Development Program, other small disadvantaged businesses, low income individuals, and firms in either labor surplus areas or areas with a high proportion of low-income individuals.

In addition, SBA provides a number of financial assistance programs for small businesses including 7(a), 504, and disaster assistance loans. Eligibility requirements vary with SBA's loan programs, surety bonds, and other programs.

GRANTS.GOV

www.grants.gov

Grants.gov allows organizations to electronically find and apply for more than $400 billion in Federal grants.

Catalog of Federal Domestic Assistance (CFDA)

www.cfda.gov

The online Catalog of Federal Domestic Assistance gives you access to a database of all Federal programs available to State and local governments (including the District of Columbia); federally-recognized Indian tribal governments: Territories (and possessions) of the United States; domestic public, quasi-public, and private profit and nonprofit organizations and institutions; specialized groups; and individuals.

Smarter Solutions

GSA, Office of Small Business Utilization
Small Business Solutions

U.S. General Services Administration
18th and F Streets, NW
Washington, DC 20405
www.gsa.gov/osbu
1-855-OSBUGSA

www.ingramcontent.com/pod-product-compliance
Lightning Source LLC
Chambersburg PA
CBHW081813280526
45789CB00008B/3120